INGABIRE M. CLAIRE

Untold Pain

DADYMINDS PUBLISHERS INSIDER

First published by DADYMINDS PUBLISHERS INSIDER 2024

Copyright © 2024 by Ingabire M. Claire

All rights reserved. No part of this publication may be reproduced, stored or transmitted in any form or by any means, electronic, mechanical, photocopying, recording, scanning, or otherwise without written permission from the publisher. It is illegal to copy this book, post it to a website, or distribute it by any other means without permission.

Ingabire M. Claire asserts the moral right to be identified as the author of this work.

Ingabire M. Claire has no responsibility for the persistence or accuracy of URLs for external or third-party Internet Websites referred to in this publication and does not guarantee that any content on such Websites is, or will remain, accurate or appropriate.

Designations used by companies to distinguish their products are often claimed as trademarks. All brand names and product names used in this book and on its cover are trade names, service marks, trademarks and registered trademarks of their respective owners. The publishers and the book are not associated with any product or vendor mentioned in this book. None of the companies referenced within the book have endorsed the book.

Learn more about the DADYMINDS Company: https://www.dadyminds.org

The Publisher: DPI (DADYMINDS PUBLISHERS INSIDER) is the TM Department in charge of book publishing and author services at DADYMINDS HOLDINGS LLC.

Email: info.dadymindsltd@gmail.com

WhatsApp: +250 (781) 355-361/+1 (307) 323-4616

Mail: 1007 North Orange Street, 4th Floor Suite #2987, Wilmington, Delaware, United States

First edition

ISBN: 979-8-33-061004-4

Editing by Anath Lee Wales

This book was professionally typeset on Reedsy.
Find out more at reedsy.com

To all those struggling with past pain and trauma, we were never promised that life would be good at all, but if you just decide to change and become a new person, I am here to convince you that healing is possible.

Contents

Preface	ii
Introduction	1
CHAPTER ONE: EFFECTS OF THE PAST	4
CHAPTER TWO: RE-DEFINING YOU AS A CROSSROAD	8
CHAPTER THREE: UNDERSTAND YOUR PAIN AND PROTECT YOURSELF	18
CHAPTER FOUR: IMPACTS	27
CHAPTER FIVE: BELIEVE YOU ARE NOT ALONE	31
CHAPTER SIX: DEALING WITH NEGATIVE THOUGHTS THAT LEAD YOU TO...	35
CHAPTER SEVEN: HUG YOUR OLD-SELF AGAIN	43
CHAPTER EIGHT: UNDERSTANDING FORGIVENESS AND ITS...	46
CHAPTER NINE: CLARIFYING WHO YOU ARE AND YOUR VALUE	50
CHAPTER TEN: LIFE BEYOND INJURY AND TRAUMA	54
CHAPTER ELEVEN: HOW TO PRACTICE PATIENCE	58
CHAPTER TWELVE; THE ROLE OF YOUR FRIENDS	61
CHAPTER THIRTEEN: EAT A HEALTHY DIET	63
CHAPTER FOURTEEN: LIVE AND BE ALIVE	65
CHAPTER FIFTEEN: YOU TOO CAN COMFORT SOMEONE	67
Conclusion	70
My Untold Story	72
About the Author	78

Preface

Every person has their history, story, and wounds. Our pasts were not our choices; everything that has happened has its reason and meaning. There is no need to continue suffering from these wounds and their consequences, as we had no part in them. Everything we did was a result of the darkness we experienced.

Dear reader, I may not know your darkness, but you need light to rediscover the brightness before you. I hope this message will help you accept and heal from the wounds of your past, allowing you to forgive those who hurt you. Above all, I wish for you to free your heart so that you can forgive yourself for your mistakes, as these mistakes can become obstacles to changing your direction.

I wish you peace of mind, happiness, and a life full of contentment.

I believe that the battles and trials we face can serve as sources of extraordinary strength on our path to success. My journey toward healing from past traumas began when I realized that the pain and trauma I experienced in childhood were not my fault. I made many mistakes, fell into countless traps, and shed many tears, which left me feeling angry at life due to guilt, constant anger, depression, anxiety, self-doubt, and persistent fear. However, through a journey of understanding who I am and why I live the way I do, I recognized that everything I struggled with was rooted in the trauma of being orphaned at a very young age, which profoundly affected my life overall.

This book results from my decision to recover from my injuries and avoid their consequences. After understanding the reasons behind my mistakes and recognizing why my life often felt dark, I chose to forgive myself and embrace who I am once again. My goal is to help those of you who are struggling with the effects of trauma on your journey to healing and accepting your wounds. I want to share my testimony, the various exercises I utilized, and the path I traversed with you—those who are still facing ongoing problems and grief. Remember to relax, stay strong, and know you are not alone. The strength and ability to confront your injuries lie within you. Recovery from severe depression and anxiety is possible, and you can learn to overcome self-doubt and regain the courage to express yourself confidently.

I hope this book will help you stop constantly blaming yourself for past mistakes and feeling sorry for yourself. It can be difficult when you feel like your life is filled with suffering, and you spend your days wondering if tomorrow will ever come or if today will ever end. This book aims to help you understand and accept the hardships you have experienced by shedding light on the reasons behind your behaviours and attitudes.

Additionally, it will offer insight into why it can be challenging to forgive those who have hurt you or to humble yourself by asking for forgiveness from those you have wronged. Most importantly, this book will help you free your heart from negative thoughts that undermine your integrity and prevent you from becoming the person you aspire to be.

Whatever you did in the past, there was something you wanted to achieve that felt right for you. Even if you made mistakes, you stood by your decisions. Whether you know or not, these actions may be connected to past injuries. I encourage you to embrace your journey and rebuild your life with compassion, trust, and mercy. You do not have to be defined by your past wounds because you are inherently brave, strong, resourceful, and fortunate.

Introduction

Experts suggest that a garden is not merely decorative; it significantly enhances the atmosphere for those who inhabit it. Those who know me know that walking through a garden is one of my favourite activities. A garden is valuable because it helps one relax, find peace and tranquillity, and meditate. Ultimately, a garden symbolizes life.

Think of your life as a garden. Just as plants need attention to thrive and be beautiful, your heart, mind, and overall health require care to flourish. The wounds you carry often stem from neglecting this inner garden, allowing negative thoughts and emotions to take root. These might include feelings of inadequacy, the pressure to please everyone, and the tendency to prioritize others' opinions over your well-being.

To cultivate a vibrant life, it's essential to remove these weeds—negative thoughts and harmful beliefs—and clear away the emotional debris. Instead, focus on planting new flowers, representing dreams and goals that inspire you. Nurture yourself, pursue joy, and prioritize self-care before trying to meet the expectations of others. Doing so can transform your life into a beautiful and fulfilling garden.

Your inner strengths—talent, knowledge, and wisdom—are like flowers, often covered by negative feelings and self-doubt. These feelings may include incompetence, worthlessness, negativity, and other harmful thoughts you direct toward yourself. Such negative emotions can lead to experiences like self-loathing, depression, constant fear, self-doubt, anger, anxiety, and other detrimental feelings. These emotions do not contribute positively to your growth, even if they stem from difficult memories in your life.

Memories can be triggered by things a person has seen, heard, or experienced without conscious awareness. Everyone carries their wounds and expresses them differently, depending on their feelings and beliefs. The same situation can hurt us all, but our scars are unique because we interpret and understand experiences differently. Therefore, it's important not to judge others too quickly. Instead, give your partner the benefit of the doubt, especially if you don't understand their behaviour or motivations.

Taking care of yourself is essential to improving your health, particularly your mental health since everything begins in the brain. It's reasonable to consider whether you can control the thoughts that enter your mind and the feelings that follow. Are these thoughts uplifting or discouraging? Remember that these emotions influence your actions, which can lead to positive or negative results. Ultimately, our daily lives revolve around our decisions, starting with our thoughts. That's why it's crucial to focus on our mental processes first.

Make time for exercise, hobbies, and other activities that bring you joy. Surround yourself with supportive friends and concentrate on the positives rather than your weaknesses. The goal is to lead a healthy life filled with joy and peace. If you invest this time in yourself, your life will flourish, and positivity will draw others to you.

In this book, I share my journey to become who I am today. I describe the steps I took and the tools I used to overcome the extreme sadness, fear, self-doubt, and anxiety that I struggled with for years. I hope you let go of your past and learn how to coexist with it—not to become stronger, but to gain the strength to live happily ever after.

Living happily doesn't mean you need to be wealthy, famous, or a leader; instead, it means being satisfied with who you are, finding peace of mind, and letting go of judgment. This book is designed to help you eliminate pain

INTRODUCTION

and sorrow, re-nourish your inner self, and allow your heart and spirit to flourish again.

CHAPTER ONE: EFFECTS OF THE PAST

Imagine living where everything you see, say, think, and touch reminds you of a past you did not choose and cannot control. For individuals who have experienced trauma, letting go of the past can be incredibly challenging. Each time they attempt to move forward, painful memories resurface, and they hear silent voices reminding them of their mistakes. This struggle often leads to feelings of depression, fear, anger, and self-blame, along with various other emotional problems. These issues are the consequences of our daily wounds, particularly when we find it difficult to accept and move on from our past experiences.

My friend, I understand that you may not realize why you're doing what you're doing or why problems seem to follow you. Sometimes, it's difficult to explain because it goes beyond your current knowledge and abilities. There are moments when you feel things beyond your imagination, and you may hesitate to express them out of fear of being judged and labelled with terms like lazy, stupid, selfish, or cruel. Many people don't know your past; they don't see the battles you're fighting in silence or the darkness you've endured. They see only the surface, unaware of the scars and wounds you carry inside.

In a study conducted by the Ministry of Health in Rwanda in 2018, it was found that at least one in five people has a mental illness. Health authorities have reported that this number has risen to almost one in five among survivors

CHAPTER ONE: EFFECTS OF THE PAST

of the genocide years after the Tutsi genocide ended.

The genocide committed against the Tutsi in Rwanda has left deep trauma, not only for the victims but also for the descendants of the perpetrators. Research by Theoneste Rutaysire and Phil Clark indicates that these descendants often experience feelings of shame and guilt due to their relatives' actions. As a result, some may change their names or relocate to distance themselves from their family's past.

It is crucial to understand that these descendants are not responsible for the crimes committed by their ancestors. They bear a burden they did not choose, and those who have been punished should not impose guilt on the next generation.

Although some people try to hide it or ignore it, the truth is that, for many of us, our lives are shaped by the injuries we have experienced. We carry heavy burdens in our hearts—grief, sorrow, tears, and a painful history—despite laughing as if we are happy on the surface. Even when we dress well and feel loved, we still bear invisible scars that prevent us from becoming the person we want or should be.

We often wonder why our love doesn't endure, why our homes face constant difficulties, why we work hard yet see little in return, why luck seems to evade us, and why our blessings are temporary. Too often, our dreams and goals linger only in our thoughts. While it may feel frustrating, it's essential to understand that failing to achieve your dreams doesn't reflect a lack of intelligence or ability. The truth is, those who succeed are just like you; they are not inherently better. The real obstacle standing in your way is the mindset that limits you.

Did you know that more than 70% of adults in the United States will experience some form of trauma at some point in their lives? Trauma is more common than we often realize, and if left unaddressed, its effects can impact all areas of our lives.

You may have gone through difficult times that left you with lasting scars, and you might still struggle with their effects. Have you lost someone you loved and accepted that your relationship has ended? Have you been betrayed and abandoned by those you trusted, including people you believed were doing everything possible to protect you? My friend, all the wounds you have faced do not define you. Your past does not define you; you are a unique individual that the world has yet to discover. You are embarking on a journey to discover what you are called to do in this world and how to heal the wounds of the past.

Constantly dwelling on the past can lead to fear, regret, self-loathing, and other daily struggles. To regain our freedom, we must heal these wounds by forgiving ourselves and those who hurt us. It's essential to understand that clinging to the past can result in failure, anxiety, depression, and a lack of hope for the future.

Before I began to recover from my injuries, I was someone who had yet to discover my true self, and I felt angry for no apparent reason. I struggled to say no, even when it meant sacrificing my happiness for others. I believed that I was doing the right thing by being a good child and adhering to biblical teachings. However, this mindset was a reflection of the trauma I had experienced. My desire to be a good child and earn the appreciation of others led some people to take advantage of me, manipulating me to satisfy their desires.

Being human, helping others, and loving are valuable traits that define us and are essential for improving the world. Our world needs good people, especially in difficult times. However, being a good person does not mean neglecting self-love and self-care. How can you truly love someone who doesn't love you back? How can you support your friends if you aren't happy yourself?

CHAPTER ONE: EFFECTS OF THE PAST

Everyone has something to give, but knowing what to focus on can be challenging when you are carrying past wounds. Prioritizing your well-being is essential, even when it's hard to ignore the voices and opinions of others. Ultimately, taking care of yourself is crucial.

It is important to remember the past but make an effort not to dwell on it. You have faced difficult times, but that challenging history does not define your life. Just as there is darkness and light, night and day, problems and solutions exist. A Good soldier earns their stripes through the tactics they use and by behaving honourably. Your wounds and experiences carry hidden meanings. Many warriors go to battle, but a true hero emerges from all they have faced. You are a unique individual, a blessing, and a hero in your own right. There is a reason why God allowed you to endure those challenges: He recognized your strength. Remember that after every storm, the light follows. Your struggles lead to a greater reward waiting for you in the future.

CHAPTER TWO: RE-DEFINING YOU AS A CROSSROAD

Educational, developmental, mental health, social, and personal traumas can lead a person to make mistakes they might regret later. If these individuals are not supported in accepting themselves and receiving the forgiveness they deserve, these mistakes can result in various problems. As they struggle with self-acceptance, feelings of anger and guilt may grow. This can lead to isolation, hatred, and, in some cases, suicidal thoughts. It is essential to understand the reasons behind these mistakes and the impact of these traumas.

Understanding the role of your experiences in grief is a crucial step in the healing process. More importantly, it's about accepting yourself and recognizing that, despite your mistakes, you are still a valuable person with significant achievements. This understanding can help you grow, become humble, and seek forgiveness from those you may have wronged. Ultimately, it will lead to relief, as self-judgment will no longer burden your heart.

You can't change the past because you can't turn back time, but the future is in your hands. Correcting mistakes and doing things differently instead of constantly blaming yourself and living in misery is possible. Taking responsibility is essential to prevent similar incidents in the future. Admitting errors allows you to recognize that change is possible. Understanding who you are and who you were before facing a difficult situation will help you

CHAPTER TWO: RE-DEFINING YOU AS A CROSSROAD

rediscover the power that lies dormant within you, enabling you to rise again and pursue your dreams.

Solange is a close friend of mine who went through a traumatic experience after breaking up with her husband of five years. When we first met her, she was a big, well-rounded woman in our lives for the last three years. I called her to ask about her health, but instead of answering me, she burst into tears and avoided making eye contact. We didn't have a long conversation; I didn't ask many questions, but I requested that she reach out to me to discuss what I needed.

It was time for Solange and me to meet in a nice, quiet spot within a beautiful garden. I noticed she avoided looking me in the face, and despite our history, we didn't leave right away. After sharing a coffee and reminiscing about our younger days, I asked about her family. She said she was doing fine, but her demeanour shifted drastically when I inquired about her husband. She seemed scared like she had just woken up from a bad dream. Realizing there was an issue, I decided to change the subject and avoid asking her further questions.

Although I changed the subject, I could see that her expression remained dark, so I approached her and said, "I'm sorry if I upset you by asking about that man." She didn't respond, but her silence suggested she was distraught, and I realized it might be serious between them. For someone who is married or in a committed relationship, betrayal is one of the most painful and destructive experiences. No one wants to be deceived in their personal life. While infidelity is often overlooked, it ignores a painful truth, and those who engage in it are acutely aware of its harm and consequences. It is considered a severe offence in both legal and religious contexts. Solange's actions fell into this category, and she understood the gravity of her actions, including the loss of value and the potential destruction of her family.

In a soft voice, I asked Solange why she had committed her crime. She explained that her husband refused to care for the house during conflicts. He would spend the night in a bar and only return home the next day. With all the money he wasted on bars and restaurants, their children couldn't go to school, were eventually thrown out of the house, and their hunger intensified.

Solange met a friend and confided in her about her struggles. The man offered her a job to help support her family. Eventually, Solange and the man ended up sleeping together. He was a widower, having lost his wife previously.

After the incident, Solange felt that her life was ruined. Even though her husband didn't care about her, she didn't want to betray him. I asked her to close her eyes and breathe slowly. As she breathed, she began to feel a sense of rest. I inquired about what she sought when she was with that man. She replied that she sought a way to care for her children. She expressed relief that her children were now studying and not going hungry.

During our conversation, she understood the reasons behind her actions, which were, in a way, understandable. I reminded her that dwelling on her sins and mistakes wouldn't be helpful. She could not go back and change what had happened; instead, she needed to take new steps and work hard to avoid repeating past mistakes. If she could avoid falling into the trap of self-harm and self-judgment, it would be best to do so.

I encouraged her to consider what truly mattered. Would she choose something that made her proud when it was revealed, or would she succumb to slander? Would she find happiness or regret later on? Taking sufficient time before making a final decision could help prevent negative consequences. If mistakes occur, accepting them and beginning anew is vital.

It is possible to start poorly and end well, but ending badly—even after a promising beginning—is ultimately a failure. It is painful and sad to start and finish poorly. In the Gospel of John, Chapter 8, Verses 3 to 7, a woman caught in adultery was brought to Jesus. The accusers believed they had the

CHAPTER TWO: RE-DEFINING YOU AS A CROSSROAD

right to stone her, as the law dictated. Instead, Jesus, writing on the ground, challenged them. They examined their sins one by one and left until only the woman and Jesus remained. This story illustrates that we all have our faults, even if we haven't been publicly confronted.

In conclusion, making mistakes and experiencing injuries are standard parts of life. Remembering your past actions is essential because you never know when your time on earth will end. Ignoring your experiences can lead you to repeat the same mistakes. The crucial question isn't what you did but rather why you did it and whether it benefited you. Focusing more on the problems or consequences of an accident rather than the lessons learned can increase your pain and potentially harm your well-being even further.

To effectively address your injuries, it's essential to take the time to fully understand their causes and what they have brought into your life. Ask yourself: Where does this anger stem from? What is the source of my jealousy and hatred? What role do I play in this life? Why am I experiencing financial difficulties? Why do I repeatedly damage my home?

Perhaps you face financial hardships because you often rely on others who may take advantage of you. You might feel compelled to please everyone, leading you to say "yes" too, which fails usually. Why do you think this need to please everyone?

By reflecting on these questions, you can realize that even if you struggle with trading and financial loss, it's not due to laziness. Instead, it may stem from a lack of strong family connections, which leads you to seek approval from others. This desire to avoid rejection can create a fear of being alone and vulnerable.

You, too, have your darkness and your nights. While some people may understand that it exists, they haven't experienced it like you have. Yes, they may sympathize with you, but you are the only one who truly feels the pain. As my friend in your struggles, remember that paradise exists, too. Do you possess something that I lack? I wish it would give you strength, for despite the darkness, there is also the sun, the moon, and the stars.

Returning to my story, I took 5 to 10 minutes to sit quietly and calm down after feeling a sense of calmness, peace, and light within myself. It was the middle of the night, and there was no noise; everyone around me sat silently. As I sat there, I began to breathe slowly, continuing to gaze at the light of the moon and the stars. After a while, a quiet voice inside me spoke, saying, "My past consists of experiences I went through without any involvement on my part." I realized that I was innocent and needed to stop fearing and blaming myself for what I did not know. I understood that I must be strong, have hope for the future, and seize all the opportunities before me. I recognized that sadness and suffering had clouded my vision, preventing me from seeing both the good and the bad. That night changed my life; it became the beginning and the catalyst for my journey to heal from the wounds of my past—wounds I did not choose and in which I had no part.

Reflecting on the realization that you are innocent is invaluable. It enables you to release unnecessary burdens and discover a sense of peace and joy, which aids in healing from past wounds that have impacted your present life. This new perspective allows you to appreciate the beautiful aspects of life overshadowed by your problems and sorrows. Additionally, it can enhance your interpersonal skills and genuine empathy, making your relationships with others more meaningful.

In summary, recognizing your loyalty aids in healing past wounds and fosters emotional and mental growth, ultimately leading to a sense of well-being. This realization reinforces your inherent strength to confront life's challenges, allowing you to lead a fulfilling life and feel content with who you are.

CHAPTER TWO: RE-DEFINING YOU AS A CROSSROAD

How can I rediscover my innocence?

It might be challenging to regain your sense of innocence after experiencing a supernatural attack, but it is possible to heal with time. One of the most accessible and effective methods for this is writing. Putting your feelings down on paper allows you to process and give importance to your emotions, acting as a window into your mind. A study from X University found that spending twenty minutes writing about their thoughts can increase their chances of healing from emotional pain by 50%. You may be unsure about what to write or how to begin.

Writing isn't the only way to help you regain confidence and acknowledge that the past has left you with wounds you didn't deserve. So, let's discuss what many call Nature. Do you ever take a moment to appreciate the good things God has created? How do you feel when you observe non-human beings, such as plants, water, animals, the sun, the moon, the stars, or the sky?

One of the things that helped me the most was my love for visiting and observing Nature. I often found solace sitting by clean lakes, watching the water flow. It reminded me that God creates without sin. The sadness and stress I experienced faded as I appreciated the beauty around me. Nature made me long to reconnect with the vibrant, green world surrounding us.

Not only is water soothing but taking a walk in the garden or the forest while listening to birds sing and watching butterflies flutter can also be incredibly relaxing for the mind. I once walked through a forest and saw trees being cut down and left to dry out. Yet, I was amazed that they eventually sprouted again, reestablishing the thickets without anyone watering or nurturing them. This made me realize that the challenges we've faced can also be overcome, similar to the trees that seem cut down but ultimately bounce back. You have helped me learn to love myself, to take care of myself, and to understand my purpose. Now, I feel more vital than ever.

Remember when you were young? The world didn't teach you that being strong meant competing with your friends. You were beautiful inside, loving everyone equally. There was no jealousy or selfishness; you were genuinely happy to share with others. You were like an angel, devoid of hate, envy, or cruelty, always believing in others as they believed in you.

Take a moment to calm down. You weren't wrong; instead, what you were taught, what others told you, what you heard, what you saw, and the people you met led you to stray from goodness. Don't let anyone think you're a coward.

Birds, plants, and water do not harbour hatred for one another; they don't always conflict as humans do, but they all want to live and thrive. The world often teaches us that honour, money, and other tangible things lead to happiness. This belief can blind us, causing us to forget that we are beings of both body and spirit. We tend to focus on our outer appearance while neglecting the inner self, the most critical aspect of our being.

While we are encouraged to work hard, as the Bible tells us, what is the point of toiling if we reap our efforts with tears? This highlights the need to care for our souls as we care for our bodies. Nurturing your soul extends your vision beyond the visible world, enabling you to gain guidance and insight about navigating life in the physical realm.

You cannot truly experience the invisible spiritual world while still immersed in the visible physical world, as they represent two opposing realms. The physical world is often marked by hypocrisy, deceit, selfishness, and a struggle for survival, while the spiritual world embodies peace, love, mutual aid, self-sacrifice, and goodwill.

Many people strive for recognition and success in the physical world, seeking fame, strength, and respect, which are evident to everyone. Conversely, those who inhabit the spiritual world are often considered foolish or despised,

CHAPTER TWO: RE-DEFINING YOU AS A CROSSROAD

as what others see as miracles may be considered trivial from a spiritual perspective.

Navigating these two realms is reasonable and necessary. However, if you are wise and prudent, placing greater emphasis on the spiritual world can enhance your understanding and experience of both. This approach allows the two worlds to complement each other, ultimately helping you become more complete.

You might wonder how I can live in this invisible world we grew up in, where our families focus on training us to be good people. Take a few minutes in the morning, around 5-10 minutes when you wake up, and at night before sleep. During these times, or whenever you find yourself alone, take a moment to talk to your heart. Try to clear your mind of distracting or painful thoughts and focus on what makes you happy and what you have achieved. This practice will help you understand who you are. Even past experiences will lose power over you because you feel like a new creation.

A Massachusetts General Hospital and Harvard Medical School study found that individuals who practised meditation and mindfulness during vacations decreased their annual medication use by 43%.

Meditation is a simple practice. Begin your day with just five minutes of meditation, focusing on your loyalty and integrity. This exercise can help you reconnect with the joyous moments of your past. Have you ever experienced a fleeting feeling that was so good and heartwarming that it seemed to ease the pain of a complicated past?

Take a moment to remember a time when you felt utterly independent and confident. What were you doing during those moments? Recall how you felt—there was peace, happiness, and contentment, even if you didn't have much formal education, a great job, or a lot of money. You might miss those days because you weren't dealing with the heartbreak you face now. Try one of the exercises I mentioned earlier, or choose another activity that could help you reconnect with your sense of innocence.

In conclusion, you cannot heal from the wounds of the past without exploring your true self. As you seek to understand your experiences, it is essential to approach this journey with understanding, compassion, and love—regardless of whether others may blame you. Reflecting, expressing your feelings through writing, spending time in Nature, and recalling the good old days when you felt more successful can help you rediscover the beauty you possessed before life's challenges altered your path. Every step to let go of guilt is a step toward freedom. Your complicated past should not define who you are but inspire you to reclaim the person you were before facing those challenges.

Rediscovering your innocence is a transformative journey that requires you to understand your past and learn how to move beyond it. To start, choose one exercise to practice tomorrow. Remember, your small steps are part of a longer journey that can help you reclaim your happiness.

As we embark on this journey together, it's essential to acknowledge that feelings of doubt, anger, and anxiety are natural for emotional beings. However, the most crucial aspect is your decision to heal. Practice forgiveness—especially towards yourself. Remember, you are not a wrong person; you are good and deserve the best in life.

Do not be afraid, for I am with you; do not be dismayed, for I am your God. I will strengthen, help, and uphold you with my righteous right hand. Isaiah 41:10-13.

The disciples asked him, "Teacher, who sinned, this man or his parents, that he was born blind?" This illustrates that sometimes, our circumstances may not directly relate to our actions. You are truly blessed if your situation is part of God's plan for you, as an incomparable blessing can arise from tears and

CHAPTER TWO: RE-DEFINING YOU AS A CROSSROAD

sorrows. However, if you recognize that there is a role you have not fulfilled, you still have the opportunity to correct your mistakes.

If you have cheated on someone you care about, seeking forgiveness is essential. While you may have reasons for your actions, the solution isn't to continue hiding but to embrace freedom by asking for their forgiveness. This process will help you feel liberated and live more freely. You'll find yourself fighting the inner turmoil that arises from this situation.

I wish you healing and the ability to forgive yourself. Just as a person can be found innocent in court after a thorough investigation, you can free your heart. Understand that everything that happens has a reason, and recognize that there is a specific desire you are trying to fulfil.

By accepting your past actions, you'll be better equipped to take new steps to prevent the same mistakes from happening again.

CHAPTER THREE: UNDERSTAND YOUR PAIN AND PROTECT YOURSELF

In Kinyarwanda, a saying is that if you want to recover from an illness, you must acknowledge it. It's essential to accept and value the thoughts and feelings associated with them to heal emotional wounds. If you feel like crying, go ahead—don't hold back. Find a quiet place and allow yourself to cry until you feel relief.

I remember how silence and the inability to express my grief weighed heavily on me. I often had headaches, and my cheeks sometimes felt swollen, as if I were carrying a heavy burden. Although I didn't understand it at the time, these were all effects of my emotional wounds.

Understanding your injuries is important because it can serve as a valuable life lesson, helping you recognize and address problems effectively. This understanding allows you to change your attitude and behaviour, which can help prevent future injuries. Acknowledging your negative feelings is crucial to accepting and healing those wounds. Deliberately ignoring or trying to escape these feelings can leave a person feeling stuck. The best way to cope with your problems is to discuss and accept them, which can help alleviate unnecessary worry.

When I was about to turn four years old, I lost my parents and my brothers,

CHAPTER THREE: UNDERSTAND YOUR PAIN AND PROTECT YOURSELF

leaving me alone in a family of eight people. My young life was turned upside down, but in 2019, it turned out to be a blessing in disguise when I separated from the father of my children and found myself alone with two kids. Although I already carried deep wounds, this separation shook me to my core. My mind and heart accepted that my life felt like nothing but pain, and I didn't expect to find happiness in this world. I felt ashamed and troubled by my situation. The injuries I carried were real and powerful. I remember walking down the street, crying and feeling utterly alone as my heart was broken.

At the beginning of 2023, I started a journey to understand who I am, why I am here, and why I constantly face challenges. It had been four years since I separated from my children's father, the man I was engaged to have children with. Yes, my family is gone; I had no role in losing it, but I wonder why I studied hard and still lost my job. Why did my family break apart so early?

Reflecting on my past, I remember being told that I was ugly and that I didn't look like my other family members. This led to feelings of rejection, and I began asking myself many questions, often being harsh and rude in my self-talk. I thought I didn't deserve the best. I even questioned whether my father was my father and if I descended from the wrong person, feeling like I had to pay for his sins. These thoughts were negative affirmations I repeated to myself to fuel my sadness.

I sought help from those who prayed to remove curses, but even when I approached witch doctors for a cure—after they said evil spirits haunted me—I found no relief.

Even though I am a mother of two children who still attend school, I found myself experiencing panic attacks, a fear of social situations, self-doubt, and insomnia once again. After trying various methods without any positive results, I encourage you to reflect on yourself as you see fit. Consider the questions: What kind of person am I? Why do I often feel like I am failing and in tears?

After dealing with curses, spells, and feelings of negativity, is it possible to overcome these challenges and find happiness again? I want to share this truth with you: you possess the power to confront the evils that lie before you because God has granted you that strength. The issue may be that you either don't recognize this power or are afraid to utilize it.

One night, unable to sleep, I woke up at eight o'clock and sat in bed. I took a pen and a notebook and began to write my story, starting from my childhood and leading up to when I became a queen. Initially, I thought only the negative experiences had marked my life, but as I wrote, I also realized there were many positive achievements.

In high school, I excelled academically and was recognized as a scholar. I also led a family within the Catholic Church and maintained good relationships with the priest. Later, I served as the Secretary General of the organization at the University of Rwanda, representing the students of the Department of Education. During that time, I felt I was succeeding.

However, life can overshadow our triumphs with trials, which have often closed my eyes to my successes. Instead, I found myself fixated on my failures and mistakes. I've understood that life is a journey of ups and downs, filled with challenges and setbacks.

That night, I sat down and read what I had written, and I felt a sense of strength and hope beginning to grow within me. Even though I was sad, I also felt happy. I realized I had more reasons to be happy than sad because most of my achievements are positive, and the negative experiences are few. I understood why I had faced challenges and recognized that I was directly or indirectly involved in those situations.

In that spirit, I went outside in the dark at the end of the month when the sky

CHAPTER THREE: UNDERSTAND YOUR PAIN AND PROTECT YOURSELF

was clear, and the light was abundant. The moon and stars glow beautifully, illuminating the world's darkness. After watching for a long time, I heard a voice whispering that although there is darkness, there is also light; although there is pain, there is also happiness; and although there is crying, laughter is also possible.

Why should I continue to focus on the troubles and dangers I've faced while ignoring the blessings that God has given me? Why dwell on the fact that I don't have parents and siblings to remember when I have a child that God has blessed me with? Why should I care about the opinions of those who say I'm wrong? Many people tell me they love and appreciate me and that I am beautiful. Even though the night sky is dark, God created the moon and stars to illuminate the world. This reminds me that the moon symbolizes fear, doubt, and alignment, while the stars represent rebirth and faith, especially for those who believe in spiritual practices like tarot. By combining these two symbols, I realize that the sky tells me my fear should disappear, allowing me to embrace a new version of myself.

This was a significant time because it allowed me to feel free again. Even though my children's father and I had been apart for four years, he kept asking for a second chance to rebuild our family. However, the wounds from our past prevented me from forgiving him. Whenever he sought forgiveness, I was overwhelmed by memories of the hurt I had experienced.

He often told me that despite the pain he caused, he still loved me and was willing to correct his mistakes to become the partner I wanted. I didn't believe a person could genuinely change, but over time, I began to see that life encompasses both good and evil. This shift in perspective helped me recall some of the good things he had done for me in the past. Despite his mistakes, I realized he had also contributed positively to my life.

After four years, we reconciled, and to this day, we have built a happy family together. I have no regrets about this journey. I feel a deep sense of accomplishment in my life, and I am grateful to my husband for his efforts in reuniting our family. He promised to marry me again, just as I wanted, and that promise was fulfilled. I am proud of him and thank God for bringing him into my life.

If I don't take a moment to reflect and make a change now, I risk living in grief or marrying another man. However, valuing my feelings has helped me choose the right partner, so it's essential to recognize and accept our emotions without running away from them or judging them. This includes being honest about feelings like anger, depression, anxiety, and fear and acknowledging that these emotions are valid.

Often, people—such as those in Rwanda—tend to express their emotions openly because some view emotional expression as akin to discarding something valuable or undergoing an abortion. Nevertheless, men often have a different experience; they may find themselves holding back their emotions, leading to a struggle. For instance, when men cry, it's usually said that their tears flow down their stomachs, symbolizing that they may repress their feelings. Many men prefer to hide their sorrow because they face stigma; those who show vulnerability are often labelled as weak, cowardly, or even failures.

Why are women allowed to express their feelings, but men often feel restricted in doing the same? Are men fundamentally different from women? If men experience feelings of love, why don't they also show sadness when things go wrong? They should be permitted to express their emotions, just like anyone else. Men are not animals; they have strong hearts and should be honest about their feelings. Their negative emotions must be valued, heard, and acknowledged, especially when facing pain or difficulties.

Understanding and accepting your wounds is an essential step toward healing. Acknowledging your pain can free your heart from judgment, allowing you to forgive those who have hurt you and reducing feelings of grief. Just like

CHAPTER THREE: UNDERSTAND YOUR PAIN AND PROTECT YOURSELF

when someone experiences an accident and visits a doctor to treat their physical wounds, emotional injuries also need to be addressed openly for proper healing.

Healing is not an instant process; it often takes time and patience. It's crucial to avoid underestimating the importance of this journey. As you work through your feelings and reflect on your experiences, you will better understand your emotions and how to manage them. Remember, every step you take now contributes to healing and helps you move forward from the wounds of your past.

What can I do to feel better and prevent injuries?

The first step to understanding your trauma is to be aware of your feelings. Just like when you are sick, when a doctor examines you and runs tests to determine what is wrong, you need to recognize and understand your emotions to figure out how to heal. For example, it's essential to differentiate between fear and anxiety, as well as between anger and jealousy or hatred, and to distinguish depression from fear. Take a moment to reflect on how you are feeling right now. What emotions are you experiencing inside?

You are reading this book because you are seeking a way to escape your current feelings. Perhaps you feel overwhelmed as if you are facing a crisis that is affecting your family, particularly your father, or you may be struggling with guilt. If you have experienced significant pain and find it difficult to forgive those feelings, take a moment to grab some paper and a pen and write it down. Whatever you're dealing with, no matter how bad or frightening it may seem, please put it on paper. Remember, you are taking care of yourself, and your feelings matter, not just for you but those around you.

Once you recognize and understand your feelings, it's essential to acknowledge that as a living person, you are expected to experience emotions when faced with unusual situations. For instance, you wouldn't simply stop feeling profound sadness after losing a friend, parent, child, or any other significant person in your life. Such losses can trigger crying, despair, and depression, and these reactions are perfectly understandable.

It's crucial to realize that these feelings exist for a reason; therefore, valuing and being willing to confront them is essential. When you feel compelled to reveal secrets shared with someone you trusted, and those secrets seem exposed to the world, it can feel like a wound. Similarly, feeling rejected by others who choose to live alone or have no one to trust is a normal response, especially if you've experienced betrayal. Your pain has meaning, and it's important to acknowledge that.

Once you understand what triggers your emotions, you can pinpoint why you feel that way. It's not a coincidence; there are specific reasons behind your feelings of anger, depression, or anxiety. As mentioned earlier, you wouldn't feel sad or seek revenge if those circumstances hadn't occurred. So, what caused you to feel this way?

I grew up wanting to be a nun, and having a family was never my dream. However, I didn't run away from the idea of a family because I was against it; instead, I was afraid. I worried that, just as I had lost my own family, I might lose another one. If that were to happen, I feared I wouldn't be able to accept it. I also worried that if my loved ones turned to God in their grief, I would be left all alone.

I often wondered if my parents and brothers would one day pass away. Would the children I might have and the man I would marry also die eventually? Fortunately, I grew up surrounded by good friends who comforted me and helped me through these dark thoughts. With their support, I overcame my fears and ultimately chose to have a family.

Looking back, I realize that my fears were justified. The loss of my family during my childhood profoundly affected me, and my feelings were rooted in

CHAPTER THREE: UNDERSTAND YOUR PAIN AND PROTECT YOURSELF

that experience. My way of thinking had a valid and apparent reason behind it.

I hope you no longer feel guilty because everything that has happened and your actions has its reasons. While those reasons may not make sense to others, they are clear and valid for you. As you understand the reasons behind your feelings, you can choose to confront them or let them be; if you feel like crying, why hold it in? Find a safe space—whether you prefer solitude or the company of someone you trust—and allow the tears to flow. When I felt sad, I often went to a quiet place alone, sitting and crying for hours. It always brought me relief. Crying is not a sign of weakness, as many believe; it takes bravery to express the pain you have endured, which can often feel overwhelming.

Writing is one of the most helpful ways I express myself. Grab a pen and paper or a notebook, and jot down everything that comes to mind. It doesn't matter if it's good or bad, a single word, a fable, or a song—just let your feelings flow! How do you feel?

What is preventing you from leading a happy life? Have you ever been told that you aren't good enough? Your feelings are valid, and what's most important is knowing how to overcome these obstacles instead of allowing them to hinder your ability to achieve the happiness and success you deserve.

Avoid injuries

Preventing injuries involves caring for your mental health, exercising regularly, getting enough rest, and learning to manage your emotions.

All the results we experience in our daily lives begin in our minds. When we send a message to the brain, it processes the information, communicates it to the heart, and interprets it as emotions. These emotions influence our behaviour, leading to actions that determine the choices we make in life.

For example, when you wake up in the morning and check the news, you might come across a story about a woman who killed her husband, and she was also married. This news can lead you to generalize and think that all women are dangerous, making you fear for your safety. This fear can create discomfort in your relationship; you may become suspicious of your partner, leading to unnecessary tension. If you're feeling uneasy, your partner will likely sense it, which could ultimately drive a wedge between you two and result in a breakup.

It's important to remember that real change in your life should start within your mind. Are your thoughts empowering you, or are they holding you back?

Physical exercise, such as walking, playing football, or swimming, helps to relax the brain by increasing blood flow. Additionally, ensuring you get enough rest, avoiding drugs, maintaining a healthy diet that includes whole grains, drinking red wine in moderation, and socializing with friends can also contribute to a relaxed mind and clearer thinking.

In conclusion, you must not ignore or run away from your feelings to find happiness again. Avoiding them only intensifies your pain. Understanding the reasons behind your emotions and allowing yourself to express them without shame or guilt will help you bear the burden that has been weighing you down for a long time. If you're struggling, seeking help from professionals who specialize in this area may be beneficial. Additionally, it's wise to protect your mind and emotions by avoiding situations that make you feel bad before they arise.

CHAPTER FOUR: IMPACTS

In addition to physical injuries and heart-related issues, it is crucial to seek medical attention for wounds that, if left untreated, can lead to severe problems, including cancer. It is essential to consult a doctor who can provide the necessary medication for healing. The doctor should cover the wound if required to ensure it heals completely. It is advised against covering an ulcer without a doctor's guidance.

The healing of physical wounds is visible to everyone; people can see them and often feel sympathy for the person affected. In contrast, heart wounds are not visible. This difference can evoke shock in others, especially if someone appears outwardly fine but is dealing with emotional pain. Regarding dental issues, some people may boast about being cured of their ailments, yet those who have sought treatment often find their new teeth breaking.

Finally, it's worth mentioning that pregnant women sometimes face stigmatization, with some people labelling them as "crazy."

Just like untreated physical injuries can lead to severe consequences, untreated heart injuries can also have grave outcomes, including the risk of losing one's life. Hiding or covering up these feelings is a form of betrayal to yourself; there is no reason to stay silent. Someone will listen to you and offer help.

The consequences of this behaviour are numerous, including self-doubt, feelings of helplessness, and a constant need for parental pampering. Such attitudes make achieving your dreams difficult and can lead to the failure of your projects, resulting in ongoing losses since you're relinquishing control over your life to others. This dependency means you often prioritize pleasing others over your own needs—feeling as though they created you and then abandoned you. Without knowing how to say no when necessary, you may find yourself being used for the benefit of others. While striving to make them happy, you might suffer in silence because you are not pursuing what you want.

Some people regularly take medication for issues like insomnia and chronic headaches, while others may rely on alcohol, cigarettes, or prescription pills. Conversely, some individuals can lie down and fall asleep immediately. If you struggle with this problem, consider finding a way to relax your mind before bedtime.

There is not only a lack of sleep but also overwhelming sadness, constant fear, and anxiety. When you fail to acknowledge your wounds to heal them and instead try to cover them up, they continually remind you of the suffering you have endured. This leads to a persistent feeling of restlessness, where even minor details disturb you, making you feel trapped in your thoughts and unsure how to make decisions or choices.

Some individuals end up taking their own lives, falling into depression, or displaying harmful behaviours. An evil person rarely laughs, even if they show care for you while also causing you pain. Some may turn into murderers, while others claim to be evil spirits. However, these so-called spirits result from deep, unresolved wounds that have festered without help, ultimately turning them into something monstrous. That's why you can never honestly know what someone is going through. Choosing your words and actions carefully is essential, as they can profoundly affect others, often without them even realizing it.

I won't claim that the effects of injuries are permanent, as each person

CHAPTER FOUR: IMPACTS

experiences trauma differently. Trauma is unique to every individual and can manifest in various ways based on their life experiences. Some people are quiet about their experiences; others are more vocal; some may laugh, while others struggle to express joy. Physically, some may become overweight as a coping mechanism, while others may focus on losing weight.

When emotional pain is not addressed correctly, it can severely impact mental, physical, and overall health. If these emotions are not adequately managed, they can lead to an increased risk of chronic diseases.

My dear friend, our daily lives are shaped by the history we have experienced together. We do not fail because we are unintelligent or cursed. The reason we seem to be stuck is not merely a period of poverty but rather a belief instilled in us since childhood: that no one in our country is born into wealth and that our fate is to live in poverty. We have come to accept this mindset. However, God did not create you to suffer; He has given you everything you need to become who you want, with some luck. What you have been enduring has robbed you of your opportunities and forced you into a life you never desired.

To prevent various side effects, it is crucial to take care of your wounds and treat them promptly to avoid serious complications, including the risk of cancer. For example, when you go to bed without addressing your wounds, you may struggle with sleep, leading to persistent headaches and low energy.

To cope with this issue, consider what activities bring you peace and happiness when you're not feeling well. Are you comfortable singing, praying, or reading a particular book? Identify what helps you relax.

Before bedtime, dedicate some time to these activities. Spend 10, 15, or even 20 minutes singing or dancing to your favourite song, praying, or reading a book you enjoy. This will help you unwind and prepare for a better night's sleep.

If stress has caused you to panic, especially before bed, consider taking a pen and paper to write down everything that happened to you that day, whether it was happy or sad. Write down your feelings without any guilt. The more you write, the more you can free your mind from those burdens. It's also beneficial to seek help by talking to friends and, if possible, consulting a mental health expert. Asking for help is a sign of courage, not weakness. In Rwanda, people say that the only way to help yourself is by giving advice and seeking support.

At the end of this chapter, the wounds that remain hidden are often accompanied by endless pain and severe consequences, including death. It is essential to value your feelings, even if they seem wrong. Understanding that these feelings have a reason is crucial; ignoring or avoiding them is akin to walking into a fire, fully aware that it will burn you and that no one will come to your aid.

It's better to acknowledge your feelings and work to resolve them to prevent further adverse effects, focusing on their root cause. Instead of trying to eliminate the symptoms, address the underlying issues. Take the first step: confront your problems and discuss them openly without fear. You have the strength within you to face your challenges; what's missing is the courage to believe that you can overcome them. Most role models we admire have gone through significant struggles, yet they dared to lead by example for their descendants, friends, and the world.

CHAPTER FIVE: BELIEVE YOU ARE NOT ALONE

I know the times you are going through are challenging, but I want to assure you that you are not alone. As someone who has experienced my share of challenges, I understand the weight of your feelings and emotions. Remember, your life is just one chapter, and although it may feel overwhelming right now, someone is always willing to listen. I am here for you.

Feeling that you are not alone can help you feel less isolated and aid in your healing process. Knowing that there are people who support you can make you realize that your life is worth living. This sense of connection allows you to share your thoughts freely, without fear and can improve your relationships with others.

When someone sees that they are not alone, it fosters hope and the belief that future situations can turn out positively, even if they have faced many losses. This mindset strengthens one's resolve to overcome challenges, instilling the understanding that they are part of a larger community, including those who have come before them and those who will follow.

Recognizing that you are not alone is crucial for healing and rebuilding. Although it is often difficult to believe that others can understand your pain during challenging times, it is indeed possible.

In 2020, after separating from the father of my children, I recalled the words of the prophets who told me I had a spirit of hatred that could hinder our progress. They warned that even if I married another man, I would not receive the blessing of a family because I had been metaphorically buried in the cemetery. The fear was overwhelming, and I felt lost. I remembered that YouTube could help people and turned to it for guidance. I realized that no one from my family remained, and I felt alone. I feared that if I saw a sibling, they would be distant and unable to comfort me. I struggled with how to explain to my children that there was no grandmother, grandfather, aunt, or uncle, and now their father was also absent.

Due to my many questions, I recalled reading various testimonies of people who had been reunited with their families after years of hardship. I often turned to a YouTube channel called Afrimax in my search for my own family, but I had little luck and discovered that they were all gone. I came across the stories of others who faced even more severe challenges than mine, and I reflected on their experiences.

Although my parents and brothers have passed away, I still have aunts and uncles. Someone was also left alone, unaware of their origins. I spoke with two others who seem like brothers, but it turns out they are in conflict, with one wanting to harm the other over property disputes. In short, everyone in this world carries a heavy burden.

Some people are burdened by poverty, while others are wealthy but restless due to chronic illnesses. Some feel sad about not having families, while others have families but feel abandoned as if they are permanently lost. This is why it's unwise to wish for someone else's life. Even if you see your partner laughing and appearing happy, they may be suffering from pneumonia that prevents them from sleeping, making you feel that your burdens are heavier than they are.

In summary, being on trial does not mean you are cursed or unworthy of

CHAPTER FIVE: BELIEVE YOU ARE NOT ALONE

the best. Many individuals we admire have experienced darkness just as you may be experiencing now, while others are enduring struggles we can't even imagine. Today, we respect these people and often aspire to emulate them.

Who do you want to be like in life? Why did you choose this person? Did they achieve something remarkable that made you look up to them? By reflecting on these questions, you'll realize that the person you admire has accomplished extraordinary things, yet they are just an average person like you. If you look closely, you'll see that they faced numerous obstacles that could have held them back, but they persevered and fought until they achieved their current success.

One effective way to help yourself is to talk to a trusted friend or family member about your problems or ideas. You might discover that another person's experiences can be more impactful than your own. This can help you realize that the challenges you're facing are not the end of the road and that change is possible. Additionally, consider joining groups or attending gatherings with others who share similar challenges, whether through sports, prayer, or specific activities. These connections can provide support and peace as you share experiences.

One way to gain courage and inspiration is by reading books, particularly those that showcase the personal lives of individuals who have faced difficult times. Their testimonies can motivate you to work hard and overcome your challenges, just as they did. If you can turn the suffering and trauma you experienced into valuable lessons, you could become an excellent role model for future generations, provided you have the strength to take action.

Let the darkness be a source of light instead of dwelling on the pain and hurtful times you have experienced. Maybe it has taught you that you cannot make everyone happy and must love and care for yourself before caring for others. Perhaps it has shown you the importance of consulting your heart before accepting and following other people's advice. While that pain is significant, it won't stop you from achieving your dreams. Remember, you are not alone; you are beautiful, capable, and worthy.

In short, it's essential to feel that you are not alone in your struggles and believe that others have endured similar challenges throughout history. Many remarkable individuals encountered extraordinary hardships but did not give up, even in the face of suffering. They drew strength from their experiences, which ultimately led them to success, and we look to them as examples in our own lives.

Additionally, if you are experiencing pain or difficulty, consider that your struggles could serve as a testament to future generations. Your perseverance can inspire your descendants to remain strong and continue fighting through their challenges. Remember, you are not alone.

Remember that gold purified in fire symbolizes that valuable things often come with significant sacrifices. If you are someone special, you may need to endure extraordinary challenges because you are destined to achieve remarkable things. God may present you with great trials so that, by overcoming them, you can support those who face similar struggles. In conclusion, I'd like to add that the scent of the stiff card inside is quite pleasant.

CHAPTER SIX: DEALING WITH NEGATIVE THOUGHTS THAT LEAD YOU TO JUDGMENT

The reason wounds continue to grow and their effects become more severe is due to the negative thoughts people harbour about their experiences. These powerful thoughts often consist of internal dialogue that differs from reality. Many people fear that history will repeat itself and believe their past defines their present and future. Past injuries frequently leave individuals with feelings of shame and guilt, leading them to question whether they were the cause of the incident or if they failed to take necessary actions. This invisible burden can make a person feel unworthy and out of place.

Managing negative thoughts and feelings of guilt can help individuals gain a new perspective, alleviating suffering and paving the way for a happier life. By addressing these issues, you can find the strength to heal from past wounds and move forward with positive thoughts. This empowerment enables you to make informed decisions and choose the right path for your life. Confronting negative thoughts is essential for achieving happiness and enjoying a long, fulfilling life.

How to deal with negative thoughts

One way to help deal with negative thoughts is to be mindful and reflective. Often, we are the ones who create our suffering through our thoughts. Consider the example of someone who doesn't accept you. It's common to feel anger and take their behaviour to heart, leading you to believe that they despise or hate you or are cruel. However, you may have no proof of these feelings. Instead, why not consider that the person may not have heard you, or perhaps they were preoccupied or dealing with their uncomfortable situation? This perspective can help you avoid spiralling into negative thoughts and protect your heart from unnecessary pain.

An example of assumptions causing distress is when you call your boyfriend multiple times, but he doesn't answer. You send him a text message, yet he still doesn't respond. Instead of considering that he might be busy or that there could be a valid reason for his silence, you may conclude that he is distancing himself from you or that someone else has taken your place. This reaction can lead to anger, but it's important to remember that your thoughts might not reflect reality. It's often better to seek clarification or wait for more information rather than make decisions based solely on uninformed assumptions. If you need to discuss something or don't understand a situation, don't expect your partner to read your mind; he is human, not omniscient.

One way to improve your mindset is to minimise time spent on external distractions such as television, social media, phone calls, and other activities. The longer you engage with these distractions, the more negative information you may absorb, which can come from unreliable sources. For instance, as a young man or woman entering the time of courtship, you might encounter stories of families who have separated, fought, or even committed violent acts against one another. Consuming such content can harm your mental well-being and instil a fear of love and establishing a home. This can lead to a belief that pursuing relationships may not be worthwhile, given what you've seen or heard. Instead, focus on dedicating more time to positive and

CHAPTER SIX: DEALING WITH NEGATIVE THOUGHTS THAT LEAD YOU TO...

enriching experiences.

If you want to navigate negative emotions, it's more beneficial to embrace a life of gratitude rather than one filled with anxiety. Even if you feel like you lack certain things, remember that you possess qualities and resources that others may desire. Please take a moment to appreciate your freedom, especially when so many at the doctor's office are on life support, wishing they could pay anything to continue living.

Even if you're experiencing difficulties, like renting a place, be grateful that you have a roof over your head. Some people are less fortunate and spend their nights outdoors. Acknowledge that you have something valuable that others might yearn for.

This doesn't mean you should stop striving for your goals and dreams. It's important to have aspirations, but if things don't unfold as expected, don't let yourself feel discouraged, as if it's the end of the world. Remember that you have done your best; this mindset can help you avoid negative thoughts.

There are several ways to manage negative thoughts. It's essential to accept that making mistakes is a natural part of life. Instead of judging yourself harshly for your mistakes, focus on learning from them. Take proactive steps to correct them and move forward.

For me, a hero has done something significant, even if it isn't recognised in newspapers or awarded with medals. My hero is my husband and the father of my children. Although we have been apart for four years and our relationship ended, he accomplished something remarkable for me. My heart has felt heavy since our breakup, and I have no intention of rekindling our relationship. This period has brought me the most pain I have ever experienced in my life.

Since we broke up, he hasn't stopped apologising to me earnestly and trying to find ways to restore our broken family. My emotional wounds have blinded me, making me fearful that responding to his requests would only bring me more pain, leading me to a week of tears and reminders of past grief. My feelings are justified because he hurt me deeply, and I can't shake the desire for him to marry another woman and find happiness elsewhere.

Despite my efforts to distance myself from him, he begged daily. As the years passed, mainly after I took the time to understand myself, I realised I was complicit in my destruction. Although I once viewed myself as an angel, my self-reflection revealed my mistakes and acknowledged the impact of my past experiences. I have been working alongside him, and while he unintentionally hurt me, he remained unaware of the consequences of his actions, believing that what he did was normal. Yet, just one word he said inflicted wounds that have lasted for over 20 years.

My husband fought tirelessly to reunite our family. It's incredible how he changed and helped me love and trust him again—something I will never fully understand. For my part, I thank God for turning our home from a place that felt like hell into a blessing. I decided to stop dwelling on his past mistakes and instead focus on the positives.

When I was pregnant with our first child, we struggled financially. I noticed our baby refused to eat so that I could have enough to survive. Seeing me cry often, my husband took it upon himself to comfort me and shared in my tears.

I recalled how he used to compare me to his birth mother, saying that he would love me despite what others thought. He chose me as his wife when many considered me unattractive, and when we were together, people often claimed we were incompatible. Some even suggested that we weren't dating and that he would be relieved to find someone else. Four years ago, he apologised to me, and I remember all we went through together. I believe he thinks positively of me because he might pursue someone else if he finds out

CHAPTER SIX: DEALING WITH NEGATIVE THOUGHTS THAT LEAD YOU TO...

we are not together. The fact that he returned to me indicates that he sees something in me that he hasn't found anywhere else.

Based on this example, you have achieved something meaningful, even if it may not be widely recognised. Think back to those sleepless nights when you felt trapped and overwhelmed. You were nervous and lacked confidence, but in the end, you persevered. Do you remember how happy you were after overcoming a long, stressful day? Have you considered where the energy and intelligence you invested during that time went? That person you were then has not changed; that person is still you. The strength you used is still within you, even if the problem seems to be resolved. Remember, you have accomplished many other things, so stop letting fear hold you back. Yes, you are capable of achieving even more.

Another way to deal with negative thoughts is by replacing them with positive ones. For example, if someone tells you that you are ugly, try not to worry about their opinion. If you're a young man and hear that no one would believe you, or if you're a girl and are told you are old or unattractive, remember that these comments do not define your worth. It's easy to accept negative feedback, primarily if you've heard it repeatedly, and it can become challenging to see your value.

You're not alone in feeling this way. I can relate to having a challenging experience during my childhood. I suffered from severe headaches, and despite my caregivers' efforts to find medication that would help, the pain persisted. It was often overwhelming and made me feel different from others. I usually found myself overthinking, especially when negative comments from my parents and relatives made me feel inadequate. My cousins and my father's family would say I was good enough, but I struggled to believe them.

It is essential to recognise that negative thoughts can stem from outside influences, but they do not have to dictate how you view yourself.

I didn't hear those words then, and I had to admit I felt terrible. I couldn't look back without physically turning around. It felt like my head was too big and heavy, so I avoided looking back. Later, I realised that the issue wasn't my big head; the overwhelming thoughts drained me. As I got older, my headaches improved because people began telling me that I had a good laugh, an appealing face, an excellent way of speaking, and even that I was beautiful.

Instead of sitting down to wonder why I'm ugly, I used to wake up in the morning and look in the mirror, look at my eyes and fingers, ask myself to hear my voice and end up smiling. Doing it often, Not just as a ritual but as something from my heart, has helped me see a beauty I never thought possible. To this day, you wouldn't say I'm ugly because I know some people see me as beautiful, and I look at myself as attractive.

So, what do you often hear from others? The most important thing is how people perceive you, but have you taken the time to reflect on how you see yourself? Have you ever been told you have "poisoned grass," meaning something is hindering your growth? Did you know that you possess the incredible power to overcome these challenges within yourself?

Perhaps you've prayed earnestly and visited the desert and the mountains but feel your prayers have gone unanswered. You might even think that God doesn't hear you. I assure you that God hears you and understands what you are experiencing. Maybe you've sought help from witch doctors or traditional healers, but they too seem to have let you down, leaving you to feel hopeless about recovery.

There is a hidden power within you that can help you navigate challenges. That power is none other than faith. The waves tossed about the ships that entered the sea because the wind was against them. Jesus approached them, walking on the water. When the disciples saw Him, they were terrified and said, "It's a ghost." However, Jesus spoke to them, saying, "Take courage; it is I. Do not be afraid."

CHAPTER SIX: DEALING WITH NEGATIVE THOUGHTS THAT LEAD YOU TO...

Peter answered, "Lord if it is you, command me to come to you on the water." "Come," Jesus replied. Peter got out of the boat and walked on the water to Jesus. But when he saw the strong wind, he became afraid and sank. He cried out, "Lord, save me!" Immediately, Jesus reached out his hand, took hold of him, and said, "O you of little faith, why did you doubt?" They got back into the boat, and the wind calmed down. Those in the boat worshipped him, saying, "Truly, you are the Son of God." (Matthew 14:22-33)

When discussing the power of faith, let's refer to Matthew 17:19-20. The disciples came to Jesus and asked, "Why were we unable to cast him out?" He replied, "Because of your little faith; for truly I tell you, if you have faith as small as a mustard seed, you can say to this mountain, 'Move from here to there,' and it will move. Nothing will be impossible for you."

Faith empowers us to replace negative thoughts with positive ones as we recognise that life is a blend of good and evil. Instead of dwelling on what harms us, we focus on what strengthens us.

Understanding that everything happens for a reason can help you cope with guilt and negative thoughts. For example, if you are invited to give a talk and, upon entering the venue, you greet the audience, what is your immediate reaction? You might think that they dislike or despise you, but often, the feelings you have about them are the opposite of how they truly feel about you. It's possible that they received instructions beforehand or might be in a difficult situation themselves. When problems arise, we blame ourselves and dwell on negative thoughts instead of seeking the truth behind the incident.

In the book "The Four Agreements" by Don Miguel Ruiz makes a point about the dangers of jumping to conclusions based on our assumptions. For example, when you pass by a group of people laughing, you might immediately think they are laughing at you when, in reality, they could be having a normal conversation. This misinterpretation often coincides with your arrival.

Much of our suffering stems from believing what is untrue. Another example is when you call your boyfriend five times, leave a message, and he doesn't answer. Instead of considering that he might be busy or dealing with another issue, you might conclude that he is rejecting you or seeing someone else. This assumption can lead to unnecessary pain.

It's important to seek clarity rather than make decisions based on incomplete information or assumptions about what is happening.

Self-blame and negative thoughts often stem from the wounds we've experienced. Engaging with art can be a powerful way to help us heal these wounds. While the scars may not fade immediately, the pain can gradually lessen, allowing us to move forward. Understanding who you are takes immense courage, as does recognising the reasons behind your wounds and being willing to confront them.

Remember that everything happens for a reason, and seeking lessons instead of dwelling on suffering can help you resist the pull of grief. Celebrate your achievements rather than focusing on your failures, as this will provide you with renewed strength to persevere. Always remember that you have the resilience to face whatever challenges come your way. You are beautiful, precious, and innocent, even in moments of hurt.

In conclusion, managing negative thoughts and guilt is a long journey but essential for our well-being. These challenges help us build confidence, enabling us to confront our perceived problems and become better individuals.

CHAPTER SEVEN: HUG YOUR OLD-SELF AGAIN

By re-embracing the past, you connect with your inner self and rediscover the values and emotions you may have lost over time. This process involves reflecting on your dreams and recalling what you wanted for your life years ago. Consider the aspirations you had that remain unfulfilled. It's an opportunity to return to that time when you felt a strong sense of talent, passion, and potential. Who did you aspire to be? Did you dream of being a soldier, a singer, a writer, or a doctor? What were your thoughts and ambitions back then?

Reflecting on your past self can be a valuable tool for anyone looking to address the wounds left by a problematic history. By doing so, you can acknowledge these wounds and gain insight into what caused them. This process can expand your mindset and help you understand the motivations behind your decisions.

Revisiting childhood memories can also reveal your talents, abilities, and strengths. This self-discovery is crucial for personal growth and healing. It's essential for your mental, emotional, and overall well-being, as it aids in recovering from emotional pain, reducing stress, improving relationships with others, and enhancing your overall sense of well-being.

Here are some ways to reconnect with your childhood: Try playing the games you enjoyed when you were young. Did you like to draw? Maybe you want to play soccer or do some handicrafts. Did you enjoy building things? What about singing or skipping rope? What was your favourite sport? No matter your age, grab a bag and play again! Find a jump rope or pick up a pencil to draw. If people laugh at you or call you crazy, remember that's a part of who you are and where your happiness lies.

One effective way to remember your childhood is to visit old landmarks or look at photographs from that time. You might consider returning to places you frequented during your youth, such as primary school or kindergarten. These visits can evoke enjoyable memories and help you reflect on your younger self. Engaging in this exercise can foster a stable relationship with yourself, allowing you to reconnect with your genuine emotions and gain a deeper understanding of who you are and how to navigate the challenging experiences you've faced.

Take a moment to close your eyes and return to your childhood, a time before sadness, hunger, worry, and tears. Remember when you played with a friend whom you considered your best? Recall the things you said freely despite the many challenges that lay ahead. You were strong and felt capable. However, as you grew up, the influences of those around you began to cloud your dreams, creating a fog that obscured your path.

I want to tell you the truth: it is still possible for your dreams to come true because the power and ability to achieve them are still within you, even if they are currently hidden. All you need to do is remove the obstacles that cover them, and your potential will shine through. Yes, it is possible because the gift lies within you.

I wish that today; you would close your ears to the discouraging sounds around you and take the time to give yourself the strength you need before facing any hurt. You will become a great singer and a remarkable queen. Don't worry about your age; focus on your dreams. Start now and make

CHAPTER SEVEN: HUG YOUR OLD-SELF AGAIN

a decision instead of waiting for tomorrow or the day after. Today marks the beginning of change, so don't let what others say affect you—prioritize yourself because life is yours alone to live.

In conclusion, reminding yourself of your dreams and goals is beneficial before confronting challenging times. This reflection allows you to recall the talents that your complex history may have overshadowed and encourages you to reawaken the abilities that circumstances have hidden. Understanding that you were born free from cruelty, hatred, and jealousy can help you let go of these negative feelings and thoughts, enabling you to become a person filled with humanity and compassion.

CHAPTER EIGHT: UNDERSTANDING FORGIVENESS AND ITS SIGNIFICANCE

Forgiveness is a conscious decision to let go of resentment and anger. It involves intentionally changing your feelings, attitudes, and behaviours so that bitterness no longer controls you, allowing you to demonstrate compassion and kindness toward those who have wronged you. Forgiveness requires an open heart to accept the mistakes of others, but most importantly, it is crucial to first forgive yourself for the pain you have endured.

Giving and asking for forgiveness requires bravery, as only the strong can perform these acts. A weak person may struggle to be humble enough to ask for forgiveness, while a proud person may find it challenging to offer it.

As God's holy and beloved people, clothe yourselves with compassion, kindness, humility, gentleness, and patience. Bear with one another and forgive each other's grievances, no matter what someone has done to another (Colossians 3:12-13). Be kind to one another and forgive each other, just as God forgave you in Christ (Ephesians 4:32).

Although forgiveness is a natural process, forgiving others and receiving their forgiveness before you can forgive yourself is often challenging. Forgiveness involves letting go of inevitable mistakes and the pain they cause by accepting what cannot be changed, learning from those mistakes, and recognizing that you made an effort even in failure. It is an act of self-love and compassion, demonstrating that, at heart, you are innocent. By forgiving, you open your heart to the light, replacing the darkness of pain with healing.

Doreen Virtue emphasized the importance of forgiving yourself for what you believe you did or didn't do. Remember, there are reasons behind the choices you made and the actions you took. You have done your best to forgive; just as you forgive your friends, it's essential to forgive yourself. If you regret learning the reasons behind their actions and genuinely want to free them from any burden, then it's crucial to ignore them—especially since your actions were justified.

Forgiveness is essential for repairing and building relationships with others. It helps to release anger and resentment, stop hatred, and prevent the desire for revenge. When you forgive, you free yourself from anger, allowing time for healing and spiritual growth.

Mercy is crucial in alleviating suffering because a person who forgives is also genuinely forgiven. By forgiving, we open our hearts and turn away from negative thoughts. Everyone should hold mercy in their hearts, as we all make mistakes and are not perfect.

How can you forgive?

Have you ever hurt someone you love and wanted their forgiveness? In that moment, you likely felt a heavy burden. You were worried and filled with fear. You might have found it hard to relax or sleep because your heart was unsettled. To start feeling normal again, you must say, "I'm sorry."

Self-reflection is a valuable technique that can help foster forgiveness. Take a moment to listen to your inner thoughts and understand your mistakes and pain. Reflecting on why these events occurred and the lessons they taught you can prevent you from dwelling on their effects, allowing you to take constructive steps toward moving forward. Additionally, choosing your words carefully when speaking to yourself is essential. Avoid using harsh language or terms that inhibit your ability to forgive.

When you engage with your inner self, approach it with the same gentleness and compassion you would offer your best friend. If you're feeling average or weak, focus on building trust within yourself. Don't rush the process; take your time and allow your feelings to guide you. Remind your mind and heart that you have the strength to do more than wait for others to validate your worth.

I once told a friend I appreciate how they laugh and have a pleasant voice. They asked me why people would lie to me about such things. I replied that many of us struggle to recognize and believe in our positive qualities; instead, we tend to focus on our flaws. It's important to understand that you possess unique advantages, and it's beneficial to acknowledge and enjoy them even before others point them out.

Living a life of gratitude for what you have can help reduce stress and regret. Acknowledge that you possess things for which others may not even dare to hope. You have a place to call home, even if you are a renter. Although you may have lost your source of income, your landlord has been patient and has not evicted you. In every challenge, there is something to be thankful for. Perhaps you have lost your job, but your children are safe at home, while others are dealing with illness or loss.

I, Claire, lost my parents and siblings when I was very young. However, I had a few close friends who became my family, and this experience has given me the gift of understanding the pain of others. If I had not lost my parents, I would not have the compassion and love I possess today. So, remember that everything happens for a reason, and God does not make mistakes. After you experience tears, take a moment to talk to yourself and ask what comes next. Instead of ignoring your feelings or running away from them, engage in conversation to discover what lessons they might teach you. I assure you, this will make you a better student.

What is keeping you from finding peace right now? Is your marriage falling apart? My friend, I understand how painful it can be when someone you trusted for years is breaking down. Ending a relationship with someone you opened your heart to can feel like a deep wound. Instead of sitting down and crying, asking, "God, what am I doing?" I turn my questions to God, seeking to understand why this is happening and how I can navigate it.

Have you thought about what might have prompted your husband or wife to want to break up? Are there responsibilities you haven't fulfilled? Can you identify what has changed within you? It's essential to explore the reasons behind these circumstances and consider what role you may have in them.

Communicate openly with your partner and see if there's anything you can do to help. Recognize that if they are unwilling to change, you cannot force it. When faced with situations that are beyond your control, sometimes the best choice is to let go and focus on things that will benefit you rather than running away from what remains.

Perhaps the person you loved did not truly love you back, and it may feel like God allowed this sadness to happen, leading to the breakup. Even in your unhappiness, I believe there is something greater that God has planned for you beyond these difficult times. Take heart and stay strong. Remember, suffering is not your inheritance.

CHAPTER NINE: CLARIFYING WHO YOU ARE AND YOUR VALUE

Have you ever wondered who you are or why you are here? It's natural to ask these questions, especially during challenging times. When you think about your identity, it's not just about your origins or knowing your parents and their lineage; it's about understanding your true self.

If you grapple with these questions, let me remind you that you are an extraordinary being. Sometimes, you might not see this because of the darkness surrounding you. Remember, only soldiers go to war, and you are one of them. You are a hero for enduring these battles. Even if you've been wounded, you have survived; you are still here.

You are unique and special, and you exist for a purpose.

You might wonder why your job feels unfulfilling despite its high salary. It's common to feel like something is missing, even if you can't pinpoint it. By reflecting on these five questions, you can clarify why you frequently switch jobs due to dissatisfaction, why you dislike what you're doing even when it seems beneficial, and why you sense something hidden within you that remains unclear.

The first question is: What do you enjoy doing in your free time? This differs

CHAPTER NINE: CLARIFYING WHO YOU ARE AND YOUR VALUE

from your job or your degree because, for example, you might have studied accounting but are currently working in education. What truly makes you happy could be activities like sewing, singing, or composing poetry. This is about something you engage in that brings you joy without needing external rewards, which you consider essential to your well-being. Is singing the most fulfilling thing in your life? I enjoy talking a lot. What about you?

The second question is: Who do you sing for? If you enjoy singing, who do you like to sing to? Is it children, loved ones, or perhaps fellow Christians?

When you observe your actions and reflect on their impact on others, you might start to question what else you are doing that could benefit them. For instance, if you enjoy sewing and you work with mothers, consider how your hobby might assist them.

What challenges are faced by individuals from the Bambara community? My contribution lies in helping them cope with the effects of their injuries. So, I encourage you to ask yourself once more: what is the purpose of what I'm doing?

Question 4 highlights additional benefits. For instance, if you enjoy singing to Christian audiences, how might your songs help them restore their faith? Perhaps your music inspires them to pray, hoping that God will hear them or provide strength during their moments of depression.

I speak with individuals who have experienced trauma, guiding them to accept their past wounds and encouraging them to build a fulfilling life. If you thoughtfully consider these four questions, they can help you better understand yourself, your purpose on this earth, and how to fulfil your role.

You might wonder how to pursue your passion when many others are already doing it and consider themselves experts. Do you think there's only one artist in your country? The answer is no; many artists, each with their own fans, resonate with their unique expression. You are unique, too; people out there need your voice, and many are waiting for you to share it.

If you're thinking, "I didn't learn enough," consider this: not all education is equally valuable, especially when you have a gift. Finding a way to use that gift is essential, even if conventional jobs might not seem suitable. We often see educated individuals who struggle while others who might not have formal education thrive. The real issue isn't about lack of learning; instead, it's about having the courage to let the light within you shine.

If you enjoy making people laugh, pursuing a comedy career could be your path to success. If you feel passionate about acting in dramas, perform; you will discover your blessings when you follow your heart. Remember, you won't become well-known simply by wishing to sing or claiming that great celebrities are out there. New artists emerge every day, and their work is appreciated by many.

What do you truly enjoy doing? Who do you work for, and what do they gain from your efforts? What do you hope to achieve? Take a moment to sit down and reflect on these questions. Answer them thoughtfully and calmly, consulting your heart before sharing your thoughts with others. Trust yourself, as those outside may offer opinions based on their perspectives or may not be truthful. Deep down, you know who you are.

It would be best if you didn't ask your friends about what they think you can or cannot do; instead, I encourage you to observe your abilities and determine what you can offer. What gifts or talents do you have that you can be confident in? How can you utilize these gifts effectively?

If you're searching for a job or feeling uncertain about your path, remember that you possess valuable qualities within yourself that can help you achieve your dreams. Don't let the opinions of others discourage you. Focus on your goals and aspirations, and believe in your ability to succeed.

CHAPTER NINE: CLARIFYING WHO YOU ARE AND YOUR VALUE

Knowing your true self and value will empower you to rise in creativity and life, enabling you to fulfil your responsibilities on earth.

On the other hand, knowing your worth means understanding your values. What is essential to you should be consistent with your principles and values.

CHAPTER TEN: LIFE BEYOND INJURY AND TRAUMA

In French, there is a proverb that says, "Après la pluie, c'est le bon temps." In English, this translates to "After the rain, there is light." This means that while we may experience trials and tribulations that feel permanent, bad times will eventually give way to good times. Just as good times come and are to be enjoyed, we must also acknowledge that bad times will pass, and good times will return.

Living beyond our wounds is a journey of healing. It involves growing beyond our struggles and recognizing that we must strive to live well despite our challenges.

Understanding that living life entirely is crucial because it helps you appreciate your existence meaningfully. Unlike a life dominated by feelings of shock, trauma, or irrational thoughts, a fulfilling life acknowledges your wounds and does not ignore them. When you recognize that your pain has significance and a clear source, it allows you to process your need to hurt, cry, and worry. This understanding can prevent you from judging yourself or feeling the need to present a false version of who you are.

To achieve success, it is essential to have a goal. Setting a goal is crucial in life because it provides direction. When you have a goal, you dedicate yourself to achieving it. This focus helps you move beyond immediate problems or past

CHAPTER TEN: LIFE BEYOND INJURY AND TRAUMA

setbacks and encourages you to achieve your objectives. Instead of dwelling on the past, you concentrate on your future. This shift in mindset prevents past experiences from wasting your time, allowing you to remain motivated and driven toward your aspirations.

Do you want to overcome a life filled with constant anxiety and tears? Do you aspire to live a happy life not defined by your past but instead focus on preventing it from happening again? If so, set a goal and declare, "I want to achieve something starting today." Even if you've been told you are slow or feel like you won't accomplish anything right now, express your thoughts and feelings about making a change and committing to that goal.

It's important to remember that simply setting goals will not lead you to success; achieving them requires hard work and dedication. You may not reach your goals on the first day, in the first month, or even in the first year. Begin with small, manageable steps and gradually increase your efforts over time.

Let's consider an example: if you want to build a house but don't have enough money, you can set a goal of saving the required amount in either five or two years. Writing down your goal and reviewing it regularly can help keep you focused and minimize distractions.

Once you have established your goal of owning a house in five years, you can break it down further. For instance, you might decide that you will have purchased a plot of land for your home in one, two, or three years. This step also requires careful planning. You could commit to saving twenty thousand rupees every month to ensure you have enough funds in time.

If you used to go out every weekend, consider reducing that to just once a month or two or three times instead. Achieving your goals often requires making sacrifices. By setting clear goals, you will spend more time thinking about the actions needed to reach them rather than dwelling on the pain and hurt of your past experiences.

Connecting with the sea and savouring its experiences is critical to truly embracing life. Taking time for self-care is essential for overall well-being. Prioritizing your body, heart, and mind is crucial. You might choose to exercise, travel to places you love, ensure you get enough rest, and engage in activities that bring you joy. Whether going out with friends, enjoying meals together, sightseeing, drawing, singing, or any other pastime, these moments contribute to your happiness.

Living with a sense of appreciation can significantly reduce pain and depression. Focusing on what you have helps shift feelings of anxiety and sadness. You may realize that you possess valuable things that can change your perspective despite not having everything you want. Confidence can drive you to work harder for what you desire.

Remember, my friend, every challenge you've faced has not defeated you; you've shown great strength by surviving those trials. Many others have faced similar struggles and unfortunately succumbed to despair, but you are still here, still fighting. So, awaken your inner strength and continue to be resilient. A better tomorrow is on the horizon; with time, you will forget the pain you've endured. You can change your story; all it takes is to stand up and take that first step toward a brighter future.

After the events in Rwanda, I never imagined that people would be able to trust and love one another again. Although they have not fully healed, Rwandans have overcome their differences and are learning to forgive each other. Today, they are getting married and supporting one another as they navigate their shared experiences. What they endured taught them about their common ancestry as Rwandans. They all strive for the development of their homeland, which helps them move beyond their wounds and choose a healthier life.

CHAPTER TEN: LIFE BEYOND INJURY AND TRAUMA

Living a life free from the burden of past wounds means committing to overcome your pain and transforming it into a source of strength for a new life. It involves letting go of negative experiences and building a brighter future. This journey requires taking control of your feelings and emotions, making intentional and stable decisions, and actively pursuing happiness and peace.

Remember that you are strong, capable, and determined to change your history and be an example to others.

CHAPTER ELEVEN: HOW TO PRACTICE PATIENCE

What is patience? How is it practised? How does it assist someone who has experienced trauma?

Resilience is the ability to endure problems, challenges, or pain without being overwhelmed. It involves navigating difficult situations effectively and acknowledging or disregarding them without harming oneself. The Bible teaches that patience leads to victory.

Patience is essential daily because it enables individuals to face problems and challenges without relying solely on defence mechanisms to make wise decisions. Patients are not hasty; instead, they remain calm and thoughtful. In contrast, an impatient person often acts impulsively, allowing anger to dictate their choices. Haste can lead to mistakes and create additional problems.

Furthermore, patience helps individuals maintain composure during difficult situations and shields their emotions from negative thoughts. When confronted with challenges, a patient takes the time to carefully evaluate the situation before making a decision, ultimately leading to better outcomes.

A manager's patience is essential for effective leadership. When a manager demonstrates patience, it helps him resolve conflicts among employees and maintain positive relationships within the team. In both work and personal

CHAPTER ELEVEN: HOW TO PRACTICE PATIENCE

life, a patient person is a blessing to friends and acquaintances. Even when faced with problems, their patience allows them to avoid rushing to judgment or reacting angrily; instead, they approach issues calmly and positively. Since we live in a world of challenges, practising patience is crucial. It enables us to remain strong and composed, even in difficult times.

How can I endure? There are many ways to develop patience, and everyone has a unique style. One effective method is exercise. Research shows that engaging in sports such as running, swimming, and football can help reduce fatigue and increase endurance. Another vital aspect is self-care. Taking time for fun and ensuring you get enough rest is essential. Additionally, looking after your overall health helps maintain your stamina.

Exercising and caring for yourself alone may not provide the strength to persevere. However, understanding your chosen strengths is essential, as it can help you avoid giving up easily. During difficult times, remember the other tough decisions you've made and the good choices that resulted from them. Recognizing that you have done your best will empower you to stay strong and persevere. You can reflect on your past successes and know you can overcome challenges.

Remember that patience is a powerful force that helps protect your heart from both minor and severe injuries. It is a crucial step in avoiding mistakes that could cause us to suffer the consequences of those injuries. Patience is not a sign of cowardice but a form of courage. If you want to manage injuries effectively, patience serves as a shield that protects your mind, heart, and life from being overwhelmed by any storm. I hope you find the strength to embrace it.

You can start trying again today in various ways, including some I've mentioned and others I haven't. For example, you could decide that when you wake up, you will do sports for twenty minutes or meditate for ten minutes. Instead of waiting for the bus or motorbike in the evening, consider walking home instead.

Let me remind you that God will not test you beyond your strength. He gave you the test of the will and chose not to provide you with children, knowing that you would excel in managing your household. Once you emerge from this experience, you will be equipped to help many married couples. Perseverance will enable you to achieve your dreams and become the person you were created to be. It will help you become a stable and exemplary individual whose testimony will inspire and support others facing similar challenges.

CHAPTER TWELVE; THE ROLE OF YOUR FRIENDS

Your friends are crucial in healing your wounds or even intensifying your pain. They can support you during challenging times by offering advice and being present to remind you that you are not alone.

The opening book of the Holy Bible states that after God created Adam, He observed that it was not good for him to be alone. Therefore, He created Eve as Adam's wife so they could spend time together, communicate, and support one another in enjoying life. This world needs each of us, and we need each other to help and complement one another. Friends and connections are crucial in our lives, but the question arises: Who are your friends? The people you spend time with or travel alongside play a significant role in your ability to heal from injuries or, conversely, to perpetuate pain. It is essential to understand the role your friends play in your life.

How do your friends or those you hang out with affect your emotions and life? Have you noticed that some always remind you of your weaknesses and vulnerabilities? Are there those who constantly bring up your painful past and make you feel stuck? How do they contribute to your journey of recovery and starting anew?

If you desire a different life than the one you're living, it's essential to surround yourself with people who inspire growth and positivity. You need individuals who can help you discover your true self and the power of your choices. It would be best to have someone who can remind you that even after hard work, there's still more to achieve. Having someone who will support and uplift you is crucial rather than bring you down again.

How do your friends support your dreams? It's not about the naysayers who claim you won't succeed; it's not about those who mock you when you're struggling and laugh at you when you're together. Consider who your mentors and friends are and how they help you from where you are and how far you've come. I'm not talking about financial support; I'm referring to thoughts, feelings, and emotions.

For example, think about your friend Kamana. You spent two years together, walking, eating, and talking. But how did Kamana meet you? What kind of person were you back then? What dreams did you have, and what role did you play in achieving those goals? As you reach milestones—20%, 30%, 70%, or even more of your dreams—you may forget Kamana's contributions to your journey. If he's no longer helping you, it might be time to reconsider your friendships. Having one good friend who supports you is far more valuable than having a thousand acquaintances who do nothing for you.

People are essential in life, but choosing friends who contribute to your growth is crucial rather than those who don't support you. This is especially important for anyone who has experienced trauma. It's vital to surround yourself with friends who make you feel good—people who are genuine, non-judgmental, and respect your feelings. Choose friends who help you move forward and heal instead of those who might hold you back.

CHAPTER THIRTEEN: EAT A HEALTHY DIET

You may wonder what a healthy diet for your mental health looks like and how it impacts your emotions. Often, we eat simply to satisfy our hunger or cravings, but it's essential to consider the implications of what we put into our bodies. The foods and drinks we consume significantly affect our thoughts, performance, emotions, and overall health. Some foods can worsen problems, while others can serve as remedies or preventive measures for issues we might face.

Nutrients like minerals and proteins are vital for the proper functioning of the body, which positively impacts brain function. Omega-3 fatty acids in fish and certain oils are essential for maintaining healthy brain activity. Additionally, reducing symptoms of mental illness, such as loneliness and anxiety, can help preserve cognitive function. A balanced diet can also help prevent consuming certain foods that may lead to headaches or stress.

For individuals who have experienced shock and trauma, it is beneficial to consume foods and beverages that support mental health and mitigate the effects of their injuries. They should focus on incorporating vegetables like broccoli and spinach and fruits such as avocados and walnuts. These foods contain essential nutrients that promote proper brain function and help reduce stress.

It is essential to include grains such as peas and nuts in your diet, as they are rich in magnesium and can help reduce the symptoms of migraines and frequent headaches. Additionally, foods high in B vitamins, like chicken, fish, and vegetables like spinach, should not be overlooked by anyone seeking good mental health, as these foods support brain function. Using vegetable oils, like avocado oil, is also beneficial for proper brain function. Finally, staying hydrated by drinking enough water is a simple yet crucial aspect of maintaining overall health.

Maintaining a healthy diet and good eating habits can help reduce mental health issues; however, if these issues persist, it is advisable to consult a specialist.

Food and drinks are not the only factors that affect anxiety. Green tea, milk, red wine, and fresh water can help you relax and alleviate excessive stress.

In conclusion, planning your diet carefully is essential, considering how it can harm or benefit your health. However, it is advisable to consult with your doctor first to ensure that the diet you choose aligns with your health conditions. Receiving medical advice as a first step is essential.

CHAPTER FOURTEEN: LIVE AND BE ALIVE

No matter your past, it doesn't change the fact that you are human; some people genuinely matter to you. When you've faced many challenges, it's common to feel overwhelmed or even as if you are losing your sense of self. This feeling is normal for anyone who has endured significant struggles. However, even if you feel insignificant, some people in your life hold meaning, whether it's your child or a dear friend. These individuals are essential to you, and they can give your life purpose. Therefore, it's necessary to continue living and to strive to be the person who has the most impact on your life and those around you.

Many believe that being necessary equates to having a lot of money and providing help in tangible or visible ways, such as clothing, food, teaching, and more. While these actions are necessary for our daily lives, it's essential to remember that basic needs like food, clothing, and sleep are not solely tied to money. Other vital aspects of life, such as Love, peace, and happiness, are equally crucial for our well-being.

Love is a gift that holds greater significance for those who believe in God, particularly Christians who trust that humanity is created in God's image. This belief suggests that we are fundamentally created in the essence of Love. Among all the commandments given to us, the one that stands above all others is LOVE.

Love is part of human nature, and although the world sometimes distorts this nature into hatred, everyone is born with an inherent capacity for Love. Who doesn't want to be loved in this world? How does it make you feel when someone important to you expresses their Love? Hearing "I love you" is a sweet refrain that brings joy to our hearts, especially when said sincerely by an adult, an elderly person, or a small child.

You are valuable. If there is someone you love, take the time to tell them often that you love them.

Just as Love does not require money, peace and happiness are essential and come at no cost. Many people have wealth but are unhappy, while others have very little yet still feel dissatisfied. To truly live and feel fulfilled, you must cultivate peace and happiness. These qualities cannot be entirely provided by anyone else; they must come from within yourself.

The peace and joy you were meant to experience are already inside you. The challenge is that suffering has obscured them, causing them to lie dormant. You might search for these feelings in your spouse, friends, or neighbours, but relying on others will not lead to complete fulfilment. Instead, look within yourself; that is where the truth resides.

Even if you weren't fortunate enough to have children, you may have a partner who loves you deeply. Every challenge you face can be seen as a miracle that brings you joy. Remember, even if others don't express it, God chose you and created you in His image, which is Love. This Love empowers you to understand that your existence is not just for the sake of Love but for God's purpose. Though you may seem insignificant in the eyes of others, in God's eyes, you are precious and essential.

CHAPTER FIFTEEN: YOU TOO CAN COMFORT SOMEONE

O ften, you may hear someone say, "Even though I am poor, I have nothing. Can you help me?" People tend to focus on money today, counting everything in monetary value. Yes, money is essential, and we need it to survive, but don't you know people who are wealthy yet very unhappy? Look closely at your friends, family, and colleagues. Are there those among them who have money but are always sad?

Some people live in nice houses but experience sleepless nights due to bad luck, while others drive nice cars but feel anxious because of credit worries. Positive encouragement, like being told you can achieve something or have value, is essential. Unfortunately, some older adults are often told they are wrong, incapable, or have nothing to contribute.

Someone needs you to hug him and feel his love because he grew up without affection and care. Perhaps he has experienced abandonment so often and feels so lonely that a simple hug could heal him, helping him regain his confidence and reconnect with his emotions. A hug is an act that requires neither money nor resources, just humanity and love. You possess these, and your embrace can make a difference in someone's life.

We often overlook the importance of cooking and the freedom it represents for individuals from families that do not provide this skill. This is why we sometimes see people—whether a queen, a pope, or an elderly individual—acting in ways that might seem immature or unconventional. It's essential to remember that their behaviour may stem from a lack of support or proper guidance in cooking, making it unfair to judge them without understanding their circumstances or background.

No one, regardless of age, wealth, strength, or vulnerability, is immune to the need for love. Love is the greatest gift you can offer to hurting someone, helping them find a reason to live again. Listening to them—even if you don't have the answers—can make a significant difference. It shows that someone is there to hear them out, allowing them to express their feelings without fear of judgment. This approach fosters trust and helps to heal their hearts.

People need to hear positive words that uplift rather than tear them down. It's important to remember that when your heart aches, your partner can also sense your pain, even if you don't want to admit it. Refrain from sharing your hurt in a way that might come across as hypocrisy, as those who are suffering can easily recognize insincerity. When they don't understand your feelings, their pain may only intensify.

Your words, gestures, and listening can save lives, and you can do this without spending any money. In Kinyarwanda, they say that a good word is a friend of God. With the fast pace of life, love and humanity are becoming increasingly rare. It can be hard to find compassion because life is expensive and demanding. However, it's essential to occasionally reach out to a friend or someone close to you and ask how they are doing. Remember, everyone is fighting their own battles in silence. This small act can show someone that there is someone who cares about them.

Additionally, let your words be comforting and healing rather than hurtful. While money can provide support, it is not the only way to help someone suffering. Your time, empathy, and love are far more valuable than anything else.

CHAPTER FIFTEEN: YOU TOO CAN COMFORT SOMEONE

May you find laughter again and reasons to keep living. May God support you and grant you the wisdom to do it right, which requires dedication.

Conclusion

He heals the brokenhearted and covers the remains of their suffering.
psalm 147;3.

For those who believe in Christ and see Him as their example, it's clear that His life was never easy in this world. He was born in a humble stable, fled to escape Herod's jealousy, and faced scorn and rejection from those who led Him to His death. He was betrayed by one of His closest followers and ultimately killed by His relatives. Despite this suffering, He is regarded as the greatest of all. His life illustrates the challenges that a true child of God can face.

My friend, you are a unique individual with exceptional talents and intelligence. You have undergone an education that prepares you for your future, and a reward awaits you. Keep fighting, and don't give up; your journey will inspire many and become stronger. Remember, you are here for a reason. While you know how long you have been on this path, you cannot predict how much time you have left in your lifetime that is not defined by the wounds or difficult experiences you have endured.

You have a reason to live, a reason to laugh again, and a reason to rise and pursue your dreams once more. This time, I hope you find extraordinary strength as you do so. Stay strong and calm through everything you've experienced.

CONCLUSION

I understand you, I love you, and I believe in you. Above all of us, there is someone who loves you more than we do, who watches over you, rejoices with you, and is always with you through both good times and bad. This being does not judge our words; He is not jealous when we come before Him. He holds everyone's life in His hands.

I see Him as a good friend, a mother, a brother, and a counsellor. Even when I felt separated from Him, His kindness followed me despite my mistakes. He never abandoned me and watched over me until I found my way back. When I returned, He did not scold or cry for me; instead, He welcomed me with the love and tenderness of a mother. There is no one other than God, the benevolent Father of us all.

The content of this book chronicles my journey through the challenges of orphanhood and the experience of loss. It reflects my path toward self-acceptance and my efforts to cope with the effects of trauma. I respect everyone's perspective, as we all interpret our experiences differently. Therefore, what is shared here is not a strict guideline but insights that may resonate with you. If you find yourself in need of additional support, remember that my doors are always open. However, if you're struggling, seeking help from a specialist is a wise choice. It's important to remember that wounds are a part of life, and while difficult times may feel overwhelming, they won't define you forever. After overcoming these challenges, you can find life and beauty once more.

My Untold Story

My name is Ingabire Marie Claire. I am a wife and a mother of two young children. I was born in May 1990 in the Gasabo district of Kigali City. I am the fifth of six children, all of whom, along with my parents, died in the 1994 genocide against the Tutsi. After their death, I was raised by my father's younger brother, whose family has been incredibly supportive of me.

I live with my wonderful family in the Kicukiro district of Kigali City. Despite my challenges, I am an ICR-certified coach, having completed the Destiny Life Coaching course in Kenya. I am also certified in the NLP & Life Coach Taster Course Level 2 by Life Practice UK Academy (The CAM Coach). Additionally, I hold a bachelor's degree in English Literature and Education from the University of Rwanda College of Education.

As I mentioned in the story, my wounds began when I was young. I grew up without parents or siblings, leading to many unanswered questions. As a child, I was quiet and focused on my studies. However, I would become angry if someone stumbled over a mistake or lied to me. I would correct them silently, which led some people to label me as a villain.

I found it hard to connect with emotions like crying and laughing. I didn't believe anyone could suffer more than I did, being without a family and not knowing what happened to them. As for laughter, I couldn't find anything amusing; whenever I saw someone laugh, it made me feel nauseous.

Growing up, I was often told that I was ugly and that I didn't look like my brothers and sisters. This constant criticism deepened my sadness and made me shy and fearful around others, to the point where I struggled to make eye contact with new people. As a result, I experienced frequent headaches and felt so heavy that it seemed difficult to lift myself. When I wanted to look back at something, I had to turn my whole body around because simply turning my head didn't change my perspective.

Why do they say I'm ugly and I don't look like my brothers? This situation challenged me, and I wondered if my mother had molested me somewhere else. Why else are they all gone, and I'm the only one left? Why am I here? These are the questions I ask myself daily, and I have no answers. My parents' families on both sides were trying to take care of me and show me love. My uncle asked me to call him "Dad," he was happy to be regarded as my father. His wife hugged me on her lap, accepting me as her child, and she became like a mother to me. However, despite their care, I couldn't shake the feeling that something was wrong. Whenever I tried to ask them about it, they would fall silent and speak to me from a distance.

One of the things that bothered me the most was not being able to see pictures of my family, as I wanted to know what they looked like. When I attended primary school, many local teachers recognized me because my mother and father had worked there before they passed away, making some sympathetic toward me. Occasionally, they would talk to me and share stories about my parents. They were kind and loving.

I became a teenager between the ages of 13 and 15 while I was at my maternal grandfather's house. One person was with me, and we were looking at pictures together. We saw a photo of a young mother sitting with three children and holding another child in her arms. Looking at the picture, I realized I didn't recognize any of them. This was the first time I asked where I had met these children and this lady.

The person I was with looked at me, and tears welled up in his eyes. However, he seemed angry, which made me feel afraid. I then asked him, "I see that you are sad. What do these people mean to you?"

He started by telling me their names, beginning with the children. However, when he mentioned the lady and said, "This is your mother," I couldn't hear anything after that. My heart ached, and a wave of fear washed over me. After a long time without knowing my family, I finally saw my mother and brothers, but that day felt like a heavy burden.

I took a photo and looked at it, noticing that the children were beautiful, just as I had been told. But at that moment, I didn't remember that I was once part of that beauty; I didn't even recognize that we shared the same blood. I eventually put the photo away and didn't mention that I had seen it because that person had forbidden me to speak about it.

I would look at a photo of my family when I missed them. If I were feeling hurt by someone, I would hug the photo and cry a lot. I was told my father was a beautiful, kind, calm man with a warm smile. I wish to know him better in the years to come. This was when the genocide against the Tutsis began.

I completed primary school and then attended Rulindo School for high school, where I studied in the Department of Languages and Literature. When I started school, my life changed significantly because I was deeply spiritual and began to read the Bible a lot. I started receiving kind words from people, telling me I had a lovely voice, a good laugh, and other compliments. As someone who mainly had heard hurtful words in the past, this support helped me break free and communicate more openly. I was beginning to believe that there was healing within me.

After finishing high school, I continued my studies at the University of Rwanda in the Department of Education, and life returned to a sense of normalcy. Nothing specifically troubled me, yet I felt a disconnect as if I was in a fog. My mind would go blank, and I was overwhelmed by a sense of forgetfulness while in school; I felt like a mere doll or figure drifting through the night. I often went to bed without eating, which led me to start drinking alcohol, believing it might help me sleep. This situation prompted me to visit a doctor, but they could not identify any underlying issues. As a result, I started trying out sleeping pills that were available for free.

At that time, I didn't even have the energy to pray and felt like I was in another world. Despite this, I somehow managed to complete my university degree. I don't fully understand how I did it. Even though I was trying to avoid teaching, some entrepreneurs recognized my efforts and agreed to work with me once I finished the course.

Life has compelled me to reflect on the past, and I find myself at the end of my journey, burdened by pain that feels ingrained in my very essence. I have sought guidance from prophets and religious figures. I have ventured into the desert and the water, hoping for God to lift the curse that weighs on me, yet life remains bitter.

In 2016, I was fortunate to meet a young man. We are now together, living as partners and making a promise in front of the law and God. Our wedding was simple, but I cherish the family we are building together, as I believe I will finally find joy in my family now.

My husband and I loved each other, and he promised me peace and love, which I desired. However, over time, what had once been love transformed into something else, and I began to regret our relationship. 2019, after only three years of marriage, we decided to break up.

This breakup hurt me deeply. I was so upset that I would walk down the street and cry. On the motorcycle, I often talked to the rider about how men can be immature, even though he hadn't done anything wrong to me. My friend, emotional pain is real and powerful. It affects everyone, regardless of how strong or wealthy they are. Even if you have experienced injuries, you often make more mistakes than if you had never stepped foot in school.

I didn't think I had a problem, so the trial was replaced by another one. As I began to reflect on my mistake, I questioned God about why I was still on earth because I wanted to go home. Do you know how to be alone without a parent, a relationship, or work? I observed this and felt troubled by its meaning, worrying that the same burden would affect my children. It is a journey marked by self-loathing and even having suicidal thoughts.

Despite everything, the children's father continued to ask me to reconcile, but his requests felt insincere. That day, I went to bed in tears, overwhelmed by memories. I still had one of his old text messages where he asked me to reconcile. From those words, it became clear that he suggested I let go of our past failures. Deep down, I struggled to believe that he had indeed changed.

In 2022, I began reflecting on myself and questioning why I was often in tears. I wanted to change my life, particularly to improve my family relationships. I started by reading books and following people on social media who had faced difficult times but emerged stronger. This process allowed me to take the time to think deeply about my situation, and I came to realize that I played a direct role in damaging my home life. My emotional wounds led me to behave in ways that pushed my partner to hurt me. He reacted to the pain I exhibited, causing harm that he hadn't intended.

The problem arose when he mentioned finding another wife, despite my belief that I was a good partner. His words seemed to imply that he found me inadequate or unsuitable, prompting me to cease communication with him. Although my husband loves me, his complex history often leads to anger and hurtful remarks. I've been encouraged to accept compliments, withstand teasing, and appreciate kind words. The experiences he conceals affect his actions in various ways.

After four years apart, we reconciled, and I am blessed that he has had time to reflect and deal with his wounds. Today, I thank God that we are a good family. When there are mistakes, we discuss them and take measures together with our children. They are happy, and we are just excited.

I praise God for giving us wisdom and direction and for taking away the remnants of the past. Although I have failed many times, suffered many times, and cried many times today, the past has no more power in my life. My future is promising, and my dreams will come true. I know I am blessed, and everything that happened has a reason. God does not make mistakes and forget that every sorrow we face has a meaning of good.

About the Author

Ingabire Marie Claire is a proud Rwandan living in the Kicukiro district of Kigali City with her wonderful family. Despite the challenges of life she has faced since She is a 1994 Rwandan Genocide against Tutsis survivor, she is an ICR-certified coach, having completed the Destiny Life Coaching course in Kenya. She is also certified in the NLP & Life Coach Taster Course Level 2 by Life Practice UK Academy (The CAM Coach). Additionally, She holds a bachelor's degree in Literature in English and Education from the University of Rwanda College of Education.

You can connect with me on:
- https://vip.dadyminds.org/author-ingabire-m-claire
- https://www.linkedin.com/in/ingabire-m-claire-3256ba62

www.ingramcontent.com/pod-product-compliance
Lightning Source LLC
LaVergne TN
LVHW052048070526
838201LV00086B/5125